PROFIT AND LOSS

PROFIT AND LOSS

Leontia Flynn

to Sarah,
with very best
wishes,

Leontia Flynn
St Paul 2013

CAPE POETRY

Published by Jonathan Cape 2011

4 6 8 10 9 7 5 3

First published in Great Britain in 2011 by
Jonathan Cape
Random House, 20 Vauxhall Bridge Road,
London SW1V 2SA

www.vintage-books.co.uk

Addresses for companies within The Random House Group Limited can be found at:
www.randomhouse.co.uk/offices.htm

The Random House Group Limited Reg. No. 954009

A CIP catalogue record for this book is available from the British Library

ISBN 9780224093439

The Random House Group Limited supports The Forest Stewardship Council (FSC®),
the leading international forest certification organisation. Our books carrying the FSC
label are printed on FSC® certified paper. FSC is the only forest certification scheme
endorsed by the leading environmental organisations, including Greenpeace.
Our paper procurement policy can be found at www.randomhouse.co.uk/environment

Typeset in Bembo by Palimpsest Book Production Limited,
Falkirk, Stirlingshire
Printed and bound in Great Britain by
MPG Books Group Ltd, Bodmin, Cornwall

CONTENTS

Part One

PART ONE

A Gothic

for Maire, Andy, Éabha and Minnie

THE DREAM HOUSE

Fourth on your list is a mid-price, brick mid-terrace
. . . what a surprise. The agent lets you in.
The first thing you see is a vase of wilted flowers
on a pot-stand, then the *Stannah* stairlift paused,
eternally it seems, up the narrow steps.

The bathroom tour confirms it. One surgical glove
lies stranded, grasping, by a beige commode.
Did the old and – ha ha ha – possibly ill
owner . . . move somewhere bigger then? you squeak.
You bolt back out to the brittle, too-bright street.

The scores on the lino, the boot-print on the door.
You thought of the ancient filth of student flats,
and of their sad and subtle narratives:
the balled-up tights retrieved from a sofa back,
the mattress flipped to show its chalky stain.

The watermarks and coffee-rings on worktops;
the wine spilled by the sofa; the low beam
where someone thought to fix a rope once; notches
on bedposts then on doorposts; errant Post-its
under old doormats, knick-knacks left in drawers.

Each loving grubby mark made by the people
over the years since one stood here, like you
and felt, with a swoop, their future being born
– as though some mythic beast in a distant land
had turned and begun its trek towards their life.

THE OVEN

It looks like a relic from another age
this *Creda* cooker, stowed in the cold back porch
of your house in Longford. Look at the eye-level grill
with the boxy handle. Look at the spooky white
of the painted oven with its pull-down door

which seems to open on a greasy tomb.
The absent cylinder plumbs it to fresh air.
When we stood that other morning on the porch
and watched the rain, two knackered-looking horses
were grazing on miles and miles of real estate.

'THE NOTORIOUS CASE OF
ROBERT THE PAINTER'

I once lived in the house of an infamous death.
Time and the tidal nature of the streets
– Baltic, Pacific, Atlantic Avenue –
had almost washed it off, but late that summer
my mother remembered hearing of the murder.

When he had choked her and hit her on the head
and stabbed her four or five times with a carving knife
the killer caught the public imagination
by scalding the woman with hot broth from the stove.
He walked away through the wire-tense post-war streets.

At night in the ashes of my own affairs
I dowsed each room for signs of macabre frisson
but the past remained dust. It would not stir at the thought
of her votive lamps, of the floor where her dentures fell,
or her roses in the garden, blooming yearly.

THE FLATS

In the first flat, up a flight of dingy stairs,
there was a sunlit room in which dust danced
and half a dead bee lay by a sash window;
where (we intoned with awe) *was the other half?*
Four or five boys smoked joints on the brown carpet.

In the second flat, the same strained air of decay
– damp on the ceiling, cigarette butts in the hearth –
but someone had wistfully added a vase filled with flowers
and a colourful throw, as though by an effort of will
the existence of rooms beside this one might be known.

In the third flat, something had gone obscenely wrong.
The plaster and paintwork were new – but a sharp smell
hung near the unpacked goods in a choked alcove.
Who, furthermore, was the figure beneath that sheet
moaning in anguish? Who watched from the lamp-less chair?

THE DOCTORS

I once lived in a house with rusted locks.
The gentleman who oversaw events
was aware of the least disturbance in each room.
He knew how Freon moved in the fridge-freezer,
that a punctured tube might shriek in a TV set.

The floors were quadrants. They mapped the past and future
like an astrological chart. He understood,
that a breeze-block lurked at the heart of the spin-drier
which stopped it in the frenzy of its cycle
from shuffling, subtly, sideways out the door . . .

REMINDERS

The bin collections and the times of Mass.
The names and dosage of prescription drugs.
My parents measure out their hours,
in this small back kitchen, regular as tides,
soothed by a filling kettle and a radio.

A fly completes a brisk Grand Prix-style circuit
around the room, then rests against the pane.
'Don't leave key in lock'
reads a note, in capitals, pinned to the back door
above the key, in the lock.

THE BULLFIGHT

When he has entered, via the Gate of Fear,
the pen of the bullring
the beast stands in indignant rage; his breath
comes and goes under the orange trees
as he begins the labour of his death.

The matador will offer him his cloak
as Veronica offered the dying Christ a cloth.
After three ritual acts, his death
running with blood, collapsing in the shade,
is met with standing cheers and gasps of breath.

After three ritual acts, his death
gasping in pain and staggering from the sun
is a *coup de grâce*, an *arte* they say – bravo! . . .
as inside the labyrinth, curled up in the shade,
the little sleeping beast flies in my womb.

INSIDE THE CATEDRAL NUEVA

Inside the Catedral Nueva in Cadiz
under the flaking dome
the saints are stood around, painted in oils,
Saints Peter, Catherine and Sebastian
posed in their tortures and their ecstasies.

The suffering here takes place in High Baroque.
My Granny in St John's
would have honoured their pierced flesh and bleeding wounds
– my granny who for twenty years or so
was stretched on the rack of her re-product-ions.

MELLARIL

Watching my uncle, restless as a child,
pacing the corridor that runs between
the kitchen and hall – all lino and chipboard paper –
if anything goes through his anguished head, I think,
it's prayers to his mother. *Requiescat in Pace*.

My uncle, alas, must take the coloured pills
morning and evening, kept in a carousel,
that ease the wild eruptions in his brain.
He wears two watches on his good right arm.
He'd like these shined with a non-abrasive agent.

Counting in sevens, rosaries, swimming pools,
swimming equipment – sports gear of *all* kinds,
my uncle likes. Dana, The Clancy Brothers,
he also likes. He likes roast meat and veg.
He likes Dean Martin and *The King and I*.

My granny, an angel, is looking down from heaven
on her son – unlucky 13th – as he furiously
turns, one-two, in the circle of himself.
On the forceps, she looks, still every moment squeezing
'too tightly' as it helps him on his way.

THE GIRL UPSTAIRS

The girl upstairs has begun once more to cry.
Her tears won't have the wild momentum of a child's.
They're regular, rhythmic; actually it's kind of soothing
to hear her sob. Outside the rising wind
rumbles the bins and makes the drinkers shout.

I know her cries will ease at one or two.
I know her movements, I know when she comes and goes
twitching the blinds or scrabbling for mail in the hall.
I know her room is haunted by the moon
of a paper lampshade. *I am the girl upstairs.*

THE DAY WE DISCOVERED
PORNOGRAPHY IN THE MAIL

I once lived in a rented red-brick house
where everyone signed on and slept till noon.
That summer, the city stood like an open door
into a room where something had just ended,
the wine glasses abandoned in the first dawn light.

Because we were so young and so belated,
because we wanted nothing and expected nobody,
the day we discovered pornography in the mail
was a revelation — it seemed a sudden windfall
or a hoopla tossed, with skill, over the rooftops.

We wanted to kneel with gentle reverence
to the envelope, where it lay behind the door
— or to take it up, like a rose, between our teeth.
We wanted to trace that name through the empty streets;
we wanted to cheer him for making a fist of it.

THE PEACE LILY
for Michael Longley

In the corner of the room the potted Peace Lily
throws up its waxy leaves towards the light.
How many grim locations around town,
passed on from friend to friend, has it called home?
It rustles – '*Hello? . . . Hello?*' – with calm neglect.

How many front rooms has the lily known?
Slamming their packed cars closed, departing friends
couldn't find space enough . . . but, look, she thrives
in the corner of the room. The potted Peace Lily
throws up her waxy flowers like spears of light.

THE VIBRATOR

When you had packed up all your books and clothes
and taken the last crap poster down, and walked
like a mournful ghost though the blank, familiar rooms,
a thought struck – clang – loud as a two-pence piece
in a metal bucket: where was the vibrator?

Oh cruel Gods! Oh vulgar implement
that was stowed discreetly on some shelf or cupboard
but has almost certainly not been boxed away . . .
Oh dirty gift of doubtful provenance.
Oh gift – surprise! – for next week's settling tenants.

Oh nice surprise for next week's settling tenants
(four Polish men paid peanuts by the hour
– for in Belfast too The Market holds its sway)
to find in some nook or niche-hole the vibrator
still beats, in the dark, its battery-powered heart.

AFTER THE FUNERAL

After the funeral and after the interment
of one of our fathers, the town where you grew up
was never so quiet – or so alien.
Where were the rusted pumps dispensing no gas to no cars?
or the Nissen hut surrounded by broken glass?

The place might have yawned like a cat in the afternoon.
Where was the school? Where the transformer station
whose hissing cups and legendary fences
– *don't kick a ball, for fuck's sake don't fly a kite* –
were stark and as un-policeable as childhood's?

THE YANKS

It's 1944 and the Yank G.I.s
now stationed at the Ballykinlar camp
regard with open mirth my father's family.
The coins they toss them strolling past the house
my granny collects and makes the kids throw back.

The Yanks toss coins. The Flynn kids throw them back
but lend the soldiers flour-bags from the store.
They learn the Yankee pop-tunes on the wireless
but scratch a swastika on the store, and fly
the Eucharistic Congress Flag at victory.

Today my father has forgotten all the words
of those old pop-tunes he used to sing his babies,
their names as well – but The Yanks loom strangely large.
He squints his sky-blue eyes across the bay
to check on their movements: their strategies and losses.

THE EXORCISM

The ghost of your former self is biding her time
at the back of the hot-press in the house where you grew
    up.
Her baneful glare is tempered by diffidence, native
to all her kind (she mouths *sorry* to the dusters, *sorry, sorry* to
    the mice).
Her interminable nights are spent watching *Father Ted*

repeated on cable, but – oh! – she hates Season Three
with its broader strokes and more formulaic deployment
of that bright, absurd wit – so spontaneous before . . .
She drums her fingers on the sofa-back.
She thinks, you know, you should make a full confession.

She thinks you should make a full and frank confession
of whatever it is that's just on the tip of your tongue.
Of whatever thing so urgently needs said
that it makes its presence felt in raps and groans
on the rails and rafters, from behind the partition wall . . .

THE HELP-LINE

At the telephone help-line in our revamped city centre
we are talking about the suicide report:
young men are opening veins, they are dropping from
   branches,
their girlfriends are swallowing tablets. What can be done,
we ask, to make life less awful here – and brief?

Behind a stand of chilly, grey, functional shelving
is my alter-ego. She is *Helen of the Phones*,
who must cradle a headset and tap a ballpoint pen
while the ghosts call up from their sealed worlds of despair.
We would like to help these spirits, Helen and I,

and to help myself – but can no more bridge the gulf
than Nicholas Hughes, the baby in the barn,
might crawl to his mother's side and will her warm.
Stand up, we urge, *from the crisis of your lives*
And exhale and look out at the new snow in the yard . . .

THE EXAMINATION ROOM

The recurring dream of the examination room
– fusty, familiar-strange with ceremony –
permits small variations. A shaft of light
might fall, through the tall hall curtains, from reinforced glass.
When we're told 'turn over your papers and begin'

the subject might be Latin? The poems of Catullus?
Multas per gentes et multa per aequora uectus
or Physics or Maths? Through a haze of years, misuse,
my tongue picks out the old mysteries: *sin*, *cos*, *tan*
like an awful ulcer – but my non-mathematical heart

is now hammering wildly. Why do the girls sit on
at their neat, square desks, like rows of cooling loaves?
And where is the clock with the bakelite face that's ticking?

When I wake it's with blind hands creeping for a pen,
hands through which, just now, time has suddenly stopped
    slipping.

TWO WAYS OF LOOKING AT AN ULTRASOUND SCAN

When the gowned technician
with the ectoplasm
offers us a glimpse of the beyond
the shadows squirm.
Is it The Turin Shroud?

Then as we lean in closer
to adjust the set
The Ghost Of All Our Christmasses to Come
appears
live! *Via* satellite!

A surveillance chart,
a CAT scan –
CCTV imagery? – a skull?
Or, as the dust settles, *nothing.*
Nothing at all.

When the weather woman
with the magic wand
gestures
to an area of high pressure
suddenly, I'm Iceland,

whose citizens
complain
they're left off so many maps
– so many maps of *Europe* –
far off, on the horizon,

where winter
is a corridor,
and pacing . . . pacing, the day
feels the lava shift, feels the whale turn,
silent, in the smoky bay.

I ONCE LIVED IN A RAILWAY
CARRIAGE FLAT

I once lived in a railway carriage flat.
I once lived in a room above the street
where yells and scraps of talk rose up like smoke.
With the first faint hoot and crash as bars let out
I hummed like a fridge, delighted, in the dark.

ANECDOTE

You find yourself suddenly very badly drunk
at a ritzy do in some renovated warehouse.
You are talking at speed to a man who's almost handsome
in a Hollywood way – except for his terrible teeth.
What's wrong with these teeth? They slant inwards like a shark's!

And this is the last clear thought you will recall
when you wake to the drama of an unknown room.
Above your head, some charming cosmic dust
spins a neutral light; there's a mystery trail
of kicked-off shoes, slumped coat, deserted jeans

that leads only, alas, to the dead-end of yourself.
You inspect a promising blister on your thumb
but the clue is cold – and so you hit the street
where some pigeons scatter – *whhhrrrpp* – at the front door's click
then, one by one, drop grimly back in place.

THE FLOPPY DISK

Prince among misnomers, the floppy disk
lies stranded, in drifts of dust, in the top desk
A castaway on shingly paper clips
or under an old bank statement – the small withdrawals
dwindling to little, then less, then nothing at all.

How young it is to be so obsolete.
The stainless-steel clip shines, the neat black case
still sleek as a woman's suit or evening purse.
I will take it between my finger and my thumb
and post it with a click through the squarish slot

of the oh-so-recent, stunningly useless past;
the moment before the moment before now
whose code is lost. The words that tapped and flashed,
like a frantic bird against a window pane,
translate back to the gesture of the hand

stalled on the keys, like the spirit on the water.
Like the shouts and groans that issue from the mine
after the prop has snapped, the floppy disk
is the love-note still sealed in its envelope.
It's the marker – blank – above its own strange grave.

THE SUPERSER

It emitted a mushroom smell.
It was mobile when empty, uselessly heavy when full.
When one or other sibling shoved it in
on wayward, squeaking wheels, the collective gasp
was the premature exit of half the room's oxygen.

It was very ugly. With hindsight, was it quite safe?
It looked like a cross between a TV robot
and a roadside shrine in Italy or France.
When I read how Lucille received the vision of hell
I deliberately toasted my toes upon its grill

just like Catholics did in books, and then drifted back
to *St Elsewhere, Dallas* or *The Antiques Roadshow*
– the upper atmosphere a roiling cloud,
our trade-off with the cold that tapped the glass,
with the shapes made out of dark – while our whole
    stunned clan

slumped safe and half-stifled on some Sunday in the
    middle of an era.

COLETTE

i.m. Séan Milne

Since her name dropped like a stone in the women's talk
I am haunted by the ghost of my mother's sister.
She comes to me out of 1939
in a little white dress and pristine Mary-Janes
clutching the gloves she'll drop on the Donegall Road.

She stoops from the kerb. The Donegall Road, *the West*,
is a disused room in my family's House of History:
the distaff wing, the city's sealed-off place.
She steps from the kerb to the not-quite-lorry-free roads
of 1940. Next year my mother is born.

Next year to the day. My mother's birthday cake
is iced in black and sweetened with black ashes;
the candle-flames are little points of dark
as dim as her dead sister's eyes that day
on the Donegall Road. The name they sang: *her* name.

Colette, Colette. My grandmother's atonement
for being so provocatively bereaved
is to lay her womb, like a flower, on heaven's altar.
The Virgin smiles and leans to soothe her brow.
After my mother, she begets seven sons.

Colette, Colette: your name is a hiccup of grief,
and the hollow knock inside an empty closet.
A seed of loss, it sprouts beyond the day
we tuck your little shoes, now yellow with age,
like a breech birth in the soil of granny's grave.

MY FATHER'S LANGUAGE

When my father sits in the straight-backed leather chair
the room contains him as my head contains this thought
of him. As though, in the gathering darkness,
made safe by the position of a rug or lamp
he is not being lost to shadows and incoherence.

As though he is not being lost to the drift of age.
Alzheimer's – slow accumulation of losses.
First, memory: the near shore of my father's life,
licked by the small waves, starts to grow faint and vague.
Next it is swept clear by the escaping tide.

First memory, then language. What process of attrition
('tangles', the text books answer, 'fatty plaques')
sees him revert to a spoken Anglo-Saxon?
His language rattles in its dearth of nouns.
Everything is a 'thing'. 'Where is the thing for the thing?'

'Where is the thing? The thing, you know, the thing?'
(In this bone-dry wasteland where the nouns have died
'daughter' might sometimes be confused with 'wife'.)
I say: *The thing's not lost. No. Take this thing.*
Here is the thing. The thing – Daddy – take this thing.

On the orange and brown linoleum lining the playroom
my infant self is playing with (that's right) dolls.
A wave of salt tenderness picks up my mum where she
    stands,
carries her off with a lurch to some far, giddy shore
then sets her back on her feet when I ask *can she whistle.*

Since my mother fell down the invisible rabbit hole
(through the isolation, hysterics and Old Wives Tales)
into stay-at-home motherhood, things have been pretty
    weird.
She regards for a beat her fat second youngest child,
then purses her lips: 'Whee-whee, whee-whee, whee-whee.

'Whee-whee, whee-whee, whee-whee, whee-whee, whee-
    whee.'
The terms in the job description clearly state
that when a small child requests whistling, you oblige.
And my epic response, when she stops to enquire just why:
Keep whistling, mummy, there's birds in my story.

Since my mother stepped through the invisible looking glass
into full-time mum-dom, each day some current frets
at her sense of self – but yes! she thinks, there are birds!
Wheeling inland, all whoops and bright hungry eyes
in the noon light, over the estuary, flying lighter than sparks.

THE DODGY PORCH LIGHT

The ancient porch light, under its plaster crown,
or plaster wreath, has been making you jump all week.
What can it mean each time you near the door
to fizz out, like some creepy plot device?
You expect a dead-eyed butler to appear

and explain *the problem's just this awful storm*
or the fuel shortage, or wires – but at heart you know
too precisely what is lurking in the dark.
The porch light flicks and fizzes when you pass.
A shadow stiffens when you turn your head.

THE PIN-HOLE CAMERA

When they had obscured the bedroom window
with king-sized towels and tablecloths, and left
just a gap, perhaps, or gape under the rail
(*look, it's not a science*); when they killed the light
the room was dark as night, and August-proofed.

And they stood there for two, three minutes till they saw
the shapes and glimmers shivering overhead
were *not* mere shadows: *Hey, isn't that a car?*
A house? A passer-by? The world outside
had beamed minutely through the black-out slit:

distorted, but moving – and in *technicolor!*
Here was the trick those old Dutch Masters used
(allegedly), and here their altered lives:
the infant slumbering in the cot, the view
interior now, bewitched and upside-down.

ROOM IN APRIL

When he had asked his friends to stay awake
and gone in the night a little way away
to think on his life and about what was to come,
the man was suddenly overcome by fear
and his heart grew sorrowful and heavy.

The hills are white, the gardens white with frost.
An icy wind cuts in along the quay
and chills the earliest Holy Week in years;
and during the longeurs of these final days of Lent
what am I reading? Poetry from the wars.

The hour is at hand. The orders have come in.
Somewhere a room whose threshold I must cross
has been prepared: an oxytocin drip
waits with the gas and air and suture tray
beside a snow-white bed. *Let this cup pass.*

PART TWO

LETTER TO FRIENDS

It's summer. So of course torrential rain
has fallen now for days; it's turned the roads
to rivers, burst the river banks, swamped drains
and drowned in a cataclysm of soupy floods
a traffic tunnel opened weeks ago.
The cars are stranded on this motorway
turned waterway – the pass is an *impasse*.
And so to pass the time I watch the slow
drip and dissolve of stuff that floats away . . .
my face is reflected in the steamy glass.

I

Recently I've been thinking of my friends
and how, when the last millennium rolled over
like an old dog, the whole world didn't end;
the slideshow function on my Mac's screensaver
shows us, uploaded, newly digitised,
fading across the distance of the screen
and each now seems an electronic ghost . . .
Things carried on. Were we, perhaps, surprised
– and are we still? What happened in between,
those and these days? What has been gained or lost?

All week it has been freezing in the flat
where – after *how* many moves? – I've had to sift
through boxes of old junk I've kept, so that
it seemed preserved, this stuff, as in a drift
of snow: old notes and diaries under ice;
photos from photo-booths – my anxious faces
glossed in IDs from universities
(strange when you hate a place to try it twice
let alone three times); all those hairstyles, phases,
freeze-frames of myriad intensities.

And strange too, how much of it is obsolete
already (though these days we're classed as *youth*
till 44). In here, among receipts
for gifts long given and lost, I've found such proof
of history's incessant forward *schlep*
picking up speed of late, as artefacts
that now seem relics from some ancient bureau.
There's (exhibit A) a 90-minute tape
filled with sad songs; a battered filofax
and some notes for countries long since using Euro.

There are fragile concertina'd inventories
for short- and long-haul flights not booked online
but in an *actual travel agent*. These
release a faint whiff of old nicotine
from trips on which assorted passengers
could while away the journey smoking fags
in designated rows, seats A, B, C . . .
(Now, though more planes – they shoot the messengers
who say so – fill the sky up with their dregs
'smoking' ranks under 'knife-crime' socially).

There's an old address book listing rented dives:
the place before the place a-place-ago
of some old friends, and weird, diminutive
phone numbers that seem missing a first 'O'
which prompts a mental trawl back through the ones
we had as kids, before successive codes
lengthened their – what? – five digits, maybe less?
And then it dawns: *there are no mobile phones*
just ancient landlines pegged along the roads,
and not a solitary email address.

There are boarding passes, rail-cards, ticket stubs.
Whether what stopped me throwing them away
was sentiment or sloth, my corny slob's
memory-hoard lets me now retrace a day
ten years ago, I caught a bus then train
(I've kept receipts of both fares – see the rings
left by my coffee on the jolting trip?)
from Edinburgh to Glasgow, back again
. . . and in between, of all the vital things,
a humbug wrapper and a hand-drawn map.

There's a photo of me drunk at Marx's grave,
a photocopied flier for a show
in Amsterdam, two giant cornflakes (they've
bleached out, gone faintly mouldy); there's a row
of smiling half-recalled contemporaries
caught, though now faded, in a Polaroid
at some event or other in the town;
there are photos of old boyfriends (number three's
absent, I note) at weddings, trips abroad,
and one in New York before the towers came down.

Here we are grinning up the Empire State
(Why are we happy? Why are we not in tears
bowed by foreknowledge?) caught between this note
which warns my student loan is in arrears,
assorted postcards pinned to flaking walls
in awful flats – Chagall, Matisse, Georges Braque –
and one unfilled *paroxetine* prescription;
there are slips from folded periodicals:
'Thanks for your short, excruciating work.
Find info enclosed (*still there*) about subscription'.

There's a desolate financial paper trail.
Follow it one way and it leads to me
un-propertied, unkempt, 'unwell' – yet still
enjoying unexpected solvency.
But trace it back the other way through slips
from temp jobs, dole-books and P45s
to summer work whose terms I can't make out,
and – hoopla – I shed myself with paperclips,
with tax and housing benefits, till I've
left myself bureaucratically quite naked.

Naked – or, worse: flayed. Flinching. Overwrought.
An insect, bolting underneath a stone
shocked by some awful hand or sudden light,
couldn't have had less functional backbone
than this sardonic-looking idiot
(me, if you're asking) propped beside a lamp,
a drink in hand at some unwholesome hour;
I want to know what makes my eyes dilate
or nostrils flare, crouched in the sweaty damp
of that old bedsit, why *stuff mattered* – for

this box of doodles, bills, old cards and prints
have meanings which are growing out of date.
I can't recall their felt significance,
like negatives developed decades late
in which we find, above all else, exposed
thwack – like a drop-kick to the heart – the gap
between our sense of *then* and of today:
no matter that the photograph was posed
or artful as the track-list of this tape
which now, I find, I have no means to play.

II

Another thing: it's hard to see just why
we got ourselves worked up into such states
(for years my chief mood was anxiety
and boredom mingled). Jesus, the debates:
the books we loved – that others must love too
or give, in writing, some good explanation,
an alibi, perhaps a doctor's note . . .
Why would I never read *Catch 22*
or Mervyn Peake? Who rated Philip Larkin,
Hal Ashby films, or what Ring Lardner wrote?

How quaint to think we few, we happy few
would to some . . . *graphic novel* yoke the fate
of getting lost round 1992
for 15 years, then figuring (too late!)
that reading stuff was, yeah, like, well and good
(I love the way our students talk today),
but we were going to need, like, some employment;
that we were going to need some livelihood,
some media job from which our minds might stray.
These days we work flat out at our enjoyment.

Indeed our ways to waste time are so many
they'd make a longer book than *Ulysses*
(whatever that is), the cacophony
of texts and tweets and emails – although these
are hardly done exclusively for pleasure
but operate like bat-squeaks in a cave
to steer us in the dark, it seems to me;
and what does a flying bat know about leisure
squeaking, perforce, from bat-birth to bat-grave?
Man can't bear too much reality (TV)

but this is our life, half virtual, half-flesh:
the instant message and the feedback loop;
the tailored advertisement made afresh
with each mouse-click – the generally crap
factoids and new-lite that we read online,
the grace of touchscreen, and the thrill unchecked
of transatlantic – trans*world* – conversation;
status updates (*Leontia's feeling fine . . .*)
squeaking across the void – 'only connect!' –
Leontia is loving all this information.

But here, though, poetry – the Holy Grail
so long – the language at its highest power,
has got its marks back from the public: fail
and fail again. The reasons for this are
a) that it's quaint and b) that it's obscure;
its flourishes and willed opacities
are verbal tics The People can't forgive.
The problem is we're not sure what it's *for* . . .
It's out of step with our capacities
for being literal – and *lucrative*

like visual art in London when it 'Shocks!'
. . . but hold on, now you'll argue that it's crass
to gauge a thing's success in earning bucks
or wish that poems be consumed *en masse*
like novels by celebrities – or booze
or rightwing tabloids sold by big tycoons
or Applications when they're bought by Apple;
I mean – is it *too much* to hope we'd choose
amid this stream of books, texts, films and tunes
some oddball words with which one has to grapple?

Yet now I find I'm falling out of line
with certain good ambassadors who state
in terms of literature we're doing fine
we've never been so keen or literate
we've never been so schooled, and only snobs
preaching apocalypse are thus inclined
to argue things are less than hunky dory,
are less than 'bright' (. . . and yet . . . and yet *a mob's
no less a mob well fed and disciplined,*
as Eliot wrote, but that's a different story).

What else is new then? Belfast, long the blight
and blot on lives has now brought to an end
or several ends, it's grim traumatic fight;
the pay-off packet and the dividend
amid the double-dealings, halts and heists:
a building boom and shopping malls thrown up
like flotsam by our new security.
Here are our palaces of snow and ice,
'and so folks with *esprit de corps* we'll shop
ourselves to civilised maturity'.

Belfast aspires to be, then, every place
where shopping is done less for recreation
(this might apply to all the western race)
than from a kind of civic obligation.
The upshot: 'on the whole we're better dressed'
as Auden wrote – though maybe on the whole
we find we suffer no less from neurosis?
Despite our retail therapy *We're Depressed,
Tired or Infertile* finds some book or poll.
Each week I hear of a fresh diagnosis

among old friends at least. It's not, I think
merely the fall-out from a far-off war
fought in our names (not so remote its stink
can't reach us in our hiding places), nor
fears for our planet that make us feel sad
(the waste, the global warming, melting ice,
our ravenous consumption of resources . . .)
though few would *gainsay* that this news is bad:
I plugged my laptop in to read it twice
such are the depths of my profound remorses.

Are we depressed that faith is in decline?
I mean the Christian faith. Except it's not
(google 'US' and 'fundamentalism'
and 'profit'). Yes, OK we've smelled the rot,
as green as grass, within the 'Church of Rome',
its awful crimes – but there are other flocks
in whom The Spirit's hardly wearing thin
so much as changing shape: it has a home
(now hear me out) in eco-politics:
for 'carbon footprint' try replacing 'sin'.

Are we depressed, then, about women's status?
Hardly, we're not quite clear who women are.
They're strong, empowered. They don't just peel potatoes.
They work, they breed, they even fight the war.
They pole-dance but they shouldn't. No, they should.
They're top consumers and they're radicals;
they're both oppressed and set free by The Veil.
(Yes, were I a student of their subjecthood
I'd find them elusive, all, as particles.)
Conversely, one hardly hears from men at all.

OK. I've said enough. It's not polite
to babble on at such prosaic length
without referring back to check you're right
behind me. (Though, conversely, that's the strength
of writing in a mostly-private mode:
it leaves you very free to bang your drum,
and preach – to empty classrooms – daring lessons.)
Forgive me. I'm surprised how fast it flowed,
or that it flowed at all. How far we've come,
or feel we've come, since our long adolescence.

III

October's been a scary month for news.
The wobble, trip and fall of several banks
had freaked us out before, across the seas,
debt spread like ripples on a ripple tank
so Auden and MacNeice out on their rambles
round Iceland (where I was a year ago)
would hardly have guessed that outpost's part was key
in all this mess: how its financial gambles,
– while global warming melts the Arctic snow –
have frozen up its whole *liquidity*.

The problem was (it seems) the price of houses
like sparks caught in an updraft, rose and rose
till men in suits decided future prices
were capital enough to sell to those
who *hadn't*, which when things went wrong spelled trouble
not just for folk left paying – through the nose –
their mortgage (which apparently means 'death grip'),
but all along the line the bursting bubble
dried up the cash, and (to mix metaphors
one last time) credit sank in the same ship.

And offering stiff competition to this strife
in fiscal matters, to the banks' collapse,
are daily threats brought to our Way of Life
by man-made imminent apocalypse
though neither really outweighs private grief
or private fears. (Last year I read *The Road*
by Cormac McCarthy up in sunny Bergen.
Now there's a romp: parental love, belief
. . . and cannibals. Oh God, I'd take the blade
to my own throat before I'd read it again . . .)

My father's wits have flown away like birds
out of that shell, though on the odd good day
watching him walk or do some task, when words
aren't called for or my thoughts drift, well then, hey,
things are just fine. Who knows? The heart that breaks
daily at each new symptom of decline
isn't my own (abstraction I can bear . . .)
and then that bubble bursts: my shoulder aches
under its flu-jab, and it strikes again
how weird it is to miss him when he's there.

What other good news from the land of grim
prognoses, where the headlines fight it out
to doom us fastest? Where, caught through the dim
nightmare of tension and of sleepless nights
(I'm talking here about new motherhood:
the grinding week-long days, the battlezone
cloaked in a fog of stunned tranquillity),
is glimpsed, on bolting out, my own dark mood
taking this form on lampposts/trees/in rain:
the single magpie looking back at me . . .

These were my thoughts while driving from the ward
under a sky perversely, brilliant blue.
What? Did the intensity of my tirade
burn off the cloud the way the sun lifts dew
to bring about this sudden climate shift
in Belfast? Look, each soot-encrusted brick
shines in a gold light, pouring from above,
celestially – so that my spirits lift
against my will. (I almost want to check,
the flood abated, for some hovering dove . . .)

A dove, an olive branch, a ray of light.
Who would have thought that only for so long
might downturns turn down; that the future's bright
and *black*? That one new Power's age-old wrong
should find redress, or symbol of redress
– and underneath her blanket with its bear
my baby daughter too now lies at ease;
she's six months old. The future's all a guess.
My heap of junk is ready for the fire;
our lives stand waiting, primed for compromise.

PART THREE

FIVE OBVIOUS CATULLUS VERSIONS

I

Let's live my arty girl and let us love
and give for the gibes and ogling of the olds
just what they're worth – approximately 1p.
Invariably the suns will fall and rise
but we have this one bright day and then no more
except for a night – the longest – to sleep through.
So give me a thousand kisses then a hundred,
And then a thousand more, then a second hundred,
And then yet another thousand-then-a-hundred.
Then when we've tallied up all these many thousands
we'll jumble up the count so *we* don't know
and no fiend can put the evil eye on us
by knowing the final sum of all our kisses.

You want to know how many of your kisses
would be enough for me – *more* than enough?
As many as the 'rich restorative' grains
of sand that lie in far-flung dream resorts,
between the fleshpots where we worship nightly
and the tourist ruins of the founding fathers.
Or as many as the stars, when a night is still,
look down upon the furtive deeds of lovers.
That's how many times I need to kiss you.
I'm mad – so that's enough, or 'more than enough'
– and it's too many for the prudes to count
or to jinx or cheapen with their wagging tongues.

3

Sparrow, my girlfriend's cherished little pet
who plays with her, who perches in her lap,
and towards whose greedy beak she might outstretch
a fingertip, soliciting a bite,
well, when on the bright coals of the burning itch
I feel for her, I tend to the jocose
— just in order, so you know, to cheer her up
and to lessen her famous spells of bitter grief —
then I'd very gladly play with her like you
and bring her some . . . *philosophical* relief.

51

4

Oh honeybunch, of boys you are *the fruit*
– not just of our own time, no, but since men were
in the beginning, are, and ever shall be . . .
I'd rather see you give the City's wealth
to him (who has no salary or savings)
than let yourself be loved by him this way.
What, isn't he *so* sweet? you ask. He is.
He's sweet and has no salary or savings.
You'll brush that off, so let me just repeat:
He hasn't any salary or savings.

Of all the coasts or coast-like shores and waters
you are the one, my watering hole, my home.
Gem on our chain of salt seas, lakes and rivers.
What joy — what a thrill! — to clap eyes on you again
(I can hardly believe them) after my inland trek
and weary progress through the landlocked cities.
And now, like a bag, the mind, exhausted, drops
Its cares on your threshold — what's lovelier than that?
And footsore and begrimed, the traveller
can collapse at last in that much-loved childhood bed;
it's what makes the awful journey all worthwhile.
It's the goal, the payoff — so now celebrate;
let the ripples in the bay be ones of laughter
let the gulls, delighted, shriek throughout the morning.

CYD CHARISSE

I

Rain on the window pane, the minor key
of Sunday afternoon, after the rote
of weekly Mass and meal. Mortality
told in the ticking clock, he'll blithely state
(although I'm only nine) or praise the flair
in *Singin' in the Rain* of Cyd Charisse.
Her apple-green chemise and blunt bobbed hair.
Her scissor legs and slow, emphatic grace.

The rain. The clock. The music and the Grace:
these are the small things I would like returned
– like an old coin long passed into circulation
pressed back in the palm – after his illness,
or the lens reversed upon his close, blurred form
to show him remote and grinning and in focus.

II

Like an old coin long passed into circulation
pressed back in the palm, at the showdown, at the end
of the day, the velvet curtain fallen,
when the old road's retraced past the final bend
to the childhood house, beyond the rusting forms
of strange machinery and sodden earth,
cowslips and hawthorn – all the long-gone farm's
half-recalled details – who'll ask, what's it worth.

That he was like this rather than like that.
How he loved music – though not monarchy
or Margaret Thatcher ('incompatible with love'
(or *Christian* love, at least, he used to say) –
small-talk at mealtimes, thoughts shared on the move,
a lifetime of priceless inconsequential chat.

A PLANE

Hydrangeas; dragons; the cave beneath a shrub.
A garden full of fading plastic toys.
Like a small, pale water-creature
fixed to a rock pool's bottom, a child looks up

beyond where a stand of huge trees circle round
to peer down, the bright fleck of a plane
is making its way across the sky's blue arc
into the beginning of memory.

BUBBLES

I comed out and I falled over . . .
You make your way, still wobbly and astonishing,
over the language's uneven ground
to blow huge bubbles at noon.
The sky is blue.

               The sky is the same bright blue
as above the weedy dunes in the endless, endless
summer of '70–what? How clear it is
– beyond the pylon and abandoned city –
that the ghost which haunts your childhood
is the ghost of my own.

               The bubbles grow.
They are irrepressible and nerve-wracking
and rainbow-smeared.
I have stood with my face pressed close
to the pane of your life.

MAGPIES

In parks, in playparks, in trees, on neighbouring fences,
on greenspace in the suburbs, on two stiff legs,
in pairs and groups – the individual magpie
perched on a chimney pot or clattering tiles . . .
Was it so near this window all this time?
Tame and banal, like half a piebald cat.

The ornithological spirit's moving poets'
imaginations to *feathered, beaked and clawed*
small endothermic bipeds. 'Of all created beings
the nearest to pure spirit', Salinger wrote –
Salinger who, since January, is dead –
naming us birders. But not the magpie – no,

the magpie wears an executioner's hood
over his vestments. Soars not, nor trills, but is witness,
like the ambulance that idles by the semi,
to the dreary goings-on behind closed doors:
the lingering death at home, say, the failed marriage.
Our buses pass on arcane schedules

their windows sheets of light against such dross
as this: the genteel drunk asleep at noon,
aged penury – and all the day's loose ends
and wisdom too . . . But not, on bins and benches,
on lampposts and on traffic islands, magpies;
on chain-mail fences bordering corner shops;

on clothes-lines and on phonewires, beside pylons,
our backyards in their sightlines – they are priests
in ones and twos, of joys and sorrows; magpies
are untranscendent and corporeal;
they are grounded. They are guardians. They keep guarded
the black and white beneath the feathers' gloss.

WEDDING WEATHER

September: the last, dry neon-headed match
left in the box soaked by long weeks of rain
makes good. A day – then two, then three days, catch...
the sky is blue as a bunsen-burner flame
and with the whiff of sea-salt, the high cries
at evening time, and late, unlikely sales
in plastic spades and buckets, come the days
long marked in diaries, cleared on schedules –
a season of surprise festivities.

The boys have had their final 'final drink'.
The girls who said *they'd never marry* are
– some of them to other girls. To think
of the effort put in just to get this far:
the venue chosen; lists; who to invite;
the card found with its quirky print – a style
agreed by both (*no hearts, no church, no white*);
the comic tune for walking down the aisle
(Darth Vader's theme?) worked so it's *them*, and *right*.

I think this is the day four thousand dawns
that faltered at the door and did not break
– or broke, in procession, on low, wintry rooms
where we slept on, at home, or where we'd wake
and be lone and whole (and missing something, true,
but not *one simple thing* we recognised
in someone else) – might yet have lead us to:
at last our inner sad selves synthesised
with those figures up there, smiling, in full view.

ACKNOWLEDGEMENTS

This book was written with the help of a major Individual Artist Award from The Arts Council of Northern Ireland.

Some of these poems have previously appeared in the following publications:

Dublin Poetry Review, Edinburgh Review, Five Dials, Five Points: a Journal of Literature and Art, From the Small Back Room: a Festschrift for Ciaran Carson, Love Poet, Carpenter: Michael Longley at Seventy, Manchester Review, New Walk, Poetry Ireland Review, Poetry London, Poetry Proper, Poetry Review, South Carolina Review: Writing Modern Ireland.

'Inside the Catedral Nueva' and 'The Bullfight' were recorded for the Poetry Archive.